Lon
Rotting On A Bookrack
by
Johnny Hart

FAWCETT GOLD MEDAL • NEW YORK

LONELINESS IS ROTTING ON A BOOKRACK

A Fawcett Gold Medal Book published by special arrangement with Field Newspaper Syndicate.

ISBN: 0-449-13942-5

Printed in the United States of America

10 9 8 7 6

7.3

7.4

RATCHET
RATCHET
RATCHET
RATCHET
RATCHET
RATCHET
RATCHET
RATCHET
RATCHET
RATCHET
RATCHET

CHUNK

7·8

WHAT'S THIS?....
I THOUGHT
BUSINESS
WAS GREAT!

FORGET IT! ....I KNOW
WHEN I'M LICKED!

7.10

RING

7-11

HELLO?

YOUR THREE MINUTES ARE UP! PLEASE DEPOSIT FOUR MORE CLAMS.

I HOPE IT'S SOME ONE I KNOW...

CHINK CHINK CHINK CHINK

7·12

SCREECH

7·13

7-14

7-17

7.19

7-20

7·22

7-24

7-27

7.29

8·1

WANNA HAND ME THAT LUG NUT?

I'D LOVE TO.

NEXT ON OUR PROGRAM....

IS A MAN WHO NEEDS NO INTRODUCTION, ...

8:3

OWING TO THE FACT THAT HE DIDN'T SHOW UP!

8·5

8·7

I NOTICED YOU WATCHING ME, ... DO YOU THINK I HAVE A FEMININE WALK?

8-8

.... HOW BOUT IF YOU TRIED IT WITHOUT DRAGGING THE BACKS OF YOUR HANDS IN THE DIRT?

8·11

8·12

8·17

YOU NEVER TAKE ME ANYWHERE.

WHERE WOULD YOU LIKE TO GO?

TO THE BEACH.

8·21

9-22

9-23

nobody loves me so I have gone away forever.

your chubby friend.

8·24

8.25

8-28

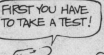

...DON'T DESPAIR, KID.

IT'S NOT WHETHER YOU WIN OR LOSE, ...IT'S HOW YOU PLAY THE GAME !

8-30

HAVE YOU EVER CONSIDERED GOING FOR A WIN ?

B
W
A
N
G

9.2

9·6

P
T
U
I

9·11

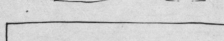

WHERE DO YOU LITTLE GREEN MEN COME FROM?

LITTLE GREEN PARENTS.

hart

9·13

9·14

RR
CROSSING

RR

TIME.

I THINK THEY'RE ON TO OUR BUNT SIGN.

9·29

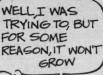

HEY MAN,...
YOU'RE GROWING
A MUSTACHE!

WELL, I WAS
TRYING TO, BUT
FOR SOME
REASON, IT WON'T
GROW

OH WOW, A MUSTACHE,
... MUSTACHES TURN
ME ON LIKE CRAZY!

MMMMMMMMMMM

10·11

10·13

10·16

UHRHH!

A GREY HAIR
IN YOUR MUSTACHE!

NOTHING REPULSES ME
MORE THAN GREY MUSTACHE
HAIRS...
EEEEOOOOUUUGHK!

10·20

OH,...ONE MORE THING
...THANKS FOR THE
GREY HAIR IN MY
MUSTACHE.

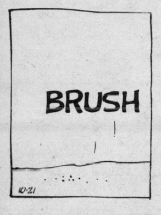

=SMACK=

10-23

WE'VE GOT TO STOP MEETING LIKE THIS.

11·2

11.3

11.4

11·6

11·21

11-23

11·24

12·21

12·22

1·2

1·3

"THIS YEAR I RESOLVE TO BECOME A VEGETARIAN!"

OH GOODY!

.... I GET TO EAT ALL THE ANTS!

1·4

DEAR GOD, COULD YOU POSSIBLY FIND IT IN YOUR HEART TO CANCEL MY RESOLVE?

1.9

THIS YEAR I PLAN TO BE LESS CLUMSY....

..AND SPEND LESS TIME STUDYING FISH...

...AND DEVOTE MORE TIME.....

TRIP ....

1-11

IN THE CREEK...

1·8

FAWCETT GOLD MEDAL BOOKS

in the B.C. series by Johnny Hart